Survival Skills

MC

Mason Crest

THE GREAT OUTDOORS!

Camping

Discovering Nature

Fishing

Hiking and Backpacking

Horseback Riding

Hunting

Mountain Biking

Snow Sports

Survival Skills

Water Sports

THE GREAT OUTDOORS! →

Survival Skills

DIANE BAILEY

Mason Crest
450 Parkway Drive, Suite D
Broomall, PA 19008
www.masoncrest.com

© 2017 by Mason Crest, an imprint of National Highlights, Inc.

Printed and bound in the United States of America.

Series ISBN: 978-1-4222-3565-2
Hardback ISBN: 978-1-4222-3574-4
EBook ISBN: 978-1-4222-8319-6

First printing
1 3 5 7 9 8 6 4 2

Produced by Shoreline Publishing Group LLC
Santa Barbara, California
Editorial Director: James Buckley Jr.
Designer: Patty Kelley
Production: Sandy Gordon
www.shorelinepublishing.com

Cover photograph: U.S. Marine Corps.

Names: Bailey, Diane, 1966- author.
Title: Survival skills / by Diane Bailey.
Description: Broomall, PA : Mason Crest, 2017. | Series: The great outdoors | Includes webography and index.
Identifiers: LCCN 2016002440| ISBN 9781422235744 (Hardback) | ISBN 9781422235652 (Series) | ISBN 9781422283196 (EBook)
Subjects: LCSH: Wilderness survival--Juvenile literature. | Survival skills--Juvenile literature.
Classification: LCC GV200.5 .B33 2017 | DDC 613.6/9--dc23
LC record available at http://lccn.loc.gov/2016002440

CONTENTS

KEY ICONS TO LOOK FOR

 Words to Understand: These words with their easy-to-understand definitions will increase the reader's understanding of the text, while building vocabulary skills.

 Sidebars: This boxed material within the main text allows readers to build knowledge, gain insights, explore possibilities, and broaden their perspectives by weaving together additional information to provide realistic and holistic perspectives.

 Research Projects: Readers are pointed toward areas of further inquiry connected to each chapter. Suggestions are provided for projects that encourage deeper research and analysis.

 Text-Dependent Questions: These questions send the reader back to the text for more careful attention to the evidence presented here.

 Series Glossary of Key Terms: This back-of-the-book glossary contains terminology used throughout this series. Words found here increase the reader's ability to read and comprehend higher-level books and articles in this field.

 Educational Videos: Readers can view videos by scanning our QR codes, providing them with additional educational content to supplement the text. Examples include news coverage, moments in history, speeches, iconic sports moments and much more!

Staying Alive

It all started when Christopher Traverse made a wrong turn. And then another. He thought he was heading south. In fact, he was traveling north, deep into the snowy wilderness of Manitoba, Canada. When his snowmobile ran out of gas 19 miles (30 km) later, Chris knew he was in trouble. He had no food. No water. No matches to start a fire. It was late in the day, and the temperature was a frigid 14 degrees F (-10 degrees C). Overhead, the sky darkened with a brewing snowstorm. He was in a battle for his survival.

Chris set to work. He used twigs and branches to build a shelter around his snowmobile. He cut the seat apart to make a pair of goggles to shield his eyes. Then he hunkered down as a blizzard howled through, bringing a foot of snow. Chris made it through that first night, but his struggle was far from over.

The next morning, Chris started to walk out. Each day he slogged through waist-deep snow for 12 hours a day. He climbed trees to see his surroundings better. That helped him figure out his location and kept him heading in the right direction. At night, he made shelters from their branches. Staying warm was critical. Chris had dressed in layers for the trip, so each day he wore only one of his two pants. That kept the other pants dry for sleeping. He knew he would get too cold if he ate snow, so he melted it before he drank it for water.

Five days later, Chris finally reached the highway and was rescued. He had almost no supplies when he got lost, but he did have two very important things that helped him through his ordeal. One was the desire to get home.

The other was the knowledge of how to survive until he did.

Sometimes survival means knowing when to call for help.

WORDS TO UNDERSTAND

bushcraft wilderness skills, named for the remote bush country of Australia

grid the large systems in society that help run it, such as power and technology

predators animals (usually large) that eat smaller or weaker animals

rewilding returning to a more natural state

CHAPTER 1

Into the Great Outdoors!

Sometimes the weather turns nasty. That marked trail? Suddenly it disappears. Someone gets hurt and now you're stranded. Campouts, fishing trips, and hikes do not always go the way they are planned. When that happens, it's a good idea to have some basic skills that will help you get through. This book can't teach every skill or cover every possibility that might happen, but it can be a guide to some important skills. You can use it as a starting point to learn more about surviving in the wild.

Ready for Anything

Survival skills get a lot of attention these days, but they are nothing new. In fact, knowing how to survive in nature has been around as long as humans have. Obviously, the earliest people did not have heated houses or canned food or electric lights. They learned to use what nature provided. Over time, people figured out easier ways to do things. As that happened, many people lost the ability to interact with nature one-on-one. Still, those skills are part of our history. They can be learned with a little bit of work.

When visiting a new place, finding expert local advice from a guide is key.

Survival boils down to a few main priorities. People have to stay warm and protect themselves from the weather and from **predators**. They have to eat and drink. They need to stay healthy and recover if they get sick or injured. It is difficult to do all these things in the middle of the wilderness, where there are few supplies or help. With a little training, though, you can learn to do the basics: start a fire, build a shelter, and get safe food and water. Then you can do the most important thing—get out!

Getting Started

Survival situations are usually not planned. That does not mean you can't plan for them. Don't get in the position of being stranded on a snowy mountaintop with no idea what to do. Instead, set up a headquarters at home to get organized. Call it your "Kitchen Command Center." This is the time to think about what skills you want to learn. Make lists of necessary items and tools, and make sure you pack them for every trip into the wilderness.

The best time to practice survival skills is when you don't really need them. It's tricky to make a roaring fire with a pile of wet wood and no matches. Hardly anyone succeeds on the first try! Wilderness schools or classes are good places to start. After that, it's a matter of practice. You may have access to some remote areas where you can try your skills. Remember that many places have strict rules. It may be illegal to hunt or start fires except under certain circumstances, even on private land. Be sure to check in advance. You do not have to "think big." If you do not have a wilderness area near your home, you might be able to use your own backyard.

You can divide your learning into steps. In a true survival situation, getting shelter would be your first priority. Building one could take several hours. In real life, you might not have that much time. You can still practice the skill, however. Work on it a little bit at a time, and take up where you left off. Even if it takes five hours spread over five days, you still have a shelter at the end. Next you have to sleep in it. How are you

Practicing wilderness skills can be a messy business—so learn to clean up after yourself! Always start fires in approved areas, and make sure you put them out fully. Do not leave trash lying around. Avoid stripping branches from live trees. In short, be careful about how you treat the natural environment. In many places, it is illegal to hunt, fish, or collect food without permission. The exception is if you are in a true survival situation. In that case, you may live off the land. It is okay to leave a trail of where you have been to help rescuers find you.

feeling halfway through the night? Is it so cold and drafty you need to go inside? If so, it is a good thing you practiced in your backyard! You can learn from your mistakes to make it better the next time. You can use this step-by-step approach for learning other skills, too.

Be Uncivilized

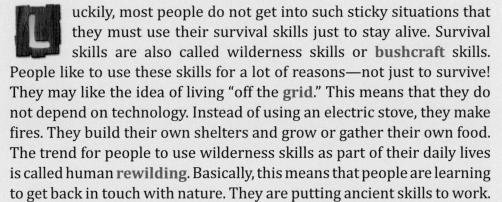

Luckily, most people do not get into such sticky situations that they must use their survival skills just to stay alive. Survival skills are also called wilderness skills or **bushcraft** skills. People like to use these skills for a lot of reasons—not just to survive! They may like the idea of living "off the **grid**." This means that they do not depend on technology. Instead of using an electric stove, they make fires. They build their own shelters and grow or gather their own food. The trend for people to use wilderness skills as part of their daily lives is called human **rewilding**. Basically, this means that people are learning to get back in touch with nature. They are putting ancient skills to work.

Only a few people do this long term. Many more could be called "weekend survivalists." They just like to go out in nature and see what they can accomplish on their own. It's a challenge—and it's fun!

TEXT-DEPENDENT QUESTIONS

1. What are two things people must protect themselves from if they are stranded in the wilderness?

2. Where are some places you can learn or practice survival skills?

3. Why do some people like human rewilding?

RESEARCH PROJECT

Find several places that teach wilderness or survival skills and compare their approaches. Which one would be the best fit for you?

Heading outdoors? Learn to read several kinds of maps.

CHAPTER 2

Getting It Done Right

n a survival situation, it all comes down to taking care of what your body needs. That means making priorities. Survivalists talk about the "Rule of Threes." A body can survive about three minutes without air. It takes three hours of cold before **hypothermia** can set in—although the odds are worse if it's windy or wet. A person can go for about three days without water. Finally, the body can last about three weeks without food.

WORDS TO UNDERSTAND

butane a type of gas used as fuel

debris hut a shelter made from scattered natural materials

friction the resistance that happens when two surfaces rub together, creating heat

hypothermia a condition where a human becomes too cold to survive

insulation protection from something, such as extreme hot or cold

Whether you are fighting for survival, or just up for a challenge, in this chapter we'll take a look at how to take care of the body's most basic needs.

Making a Shelter

I n most wilderness situations, the most important priority is to stay warm. Even in summer, the temperature can get cold at night, especially at high altitudes. Also, constant exposure to the elements saps heat from your body. If your clothes are wet, you lose heat even faster. Getting shelter is job number one.

Nature is full of temporary shelters, such as trees, caves, or rock overhangs. These will block the wind and provide some protection. It's also possible to build a shelter. A **debris hut** can be built fairly quickly, from things you find around you. Your shelter may be small and crooked, but that's okay. Small is better. The only warmth you'll have in your new house will be coming from your own body. The less space you have to heat, the warmer you will be!

First, find a spot to build it. A tree with a fork three or four feet off the ground is ideal. Next, find a fallen branch about five or six inches thick and a couple of feet longer than you are tall. Wedge it into the fork of the tree and let the other end taper to the ground. This branch is called the ridge pole. Think of it as the backbone of your shelter. If you can't find a tree to hold your branch, look around for a branch that is in the shape of a "Y." Dig a hole and "plant" the Y-shaped branch. Now you can prop the ridge pole in its fork. Next, find smaller twigs and branches and prop them up against the side of the ridge pole. These will be the ribs that go beside the backbone. Finally, fill in the spaces with leaves, moss, and any other muck you can find. This is the flesh of the shelter and provides **insulation** from the wind and cold temperatures.

A simple debris hut

Once you've built a shelter, it's time to use it. A big risk for people trapped in the wilderness is not getting enough sleep. It is difficult to sleep if you are worried and scared, but people who are tired do not function well. They do not have enough energy to do the physical tasks they need to. When they try to power through it, they end up making mistakes in their work. They also lose judgment and make bad decisions. Sleeping at night is usually best because it is too dark to see well. However, plan your sleeping around your situation. If you are in an extremely hot place, it might be better to find a shady place and catch some zz's in the afternoon, when it is too hot to work.

Different environments will require different types of shelters. There usually are not many trees or bushes in a desert, but it is still possible to find shelter in caves, next to rocks, or even under the sand. Another hostile environment is snow. It seems strange that you can live—and even stay warm!—in a snow house, but native peoples have done it for thousands of years by tunneling into the snow. All of these skills will require more research and practice, but in almost any environment, there is a way to take shelter if you know what to look for.

Starting a Fire

No other species on Earth uses fire. It is a tool exclusively for humans. Making a fire is one of the most basic survival skills. In the wild, fire can be used to provide heat and light, to cook food, and to scare off potential predators.

First, take the time to collect material that will burn well. It is frustrating to make a flame only to have it go out immediately because the fuel did not burn. You'll need a variety of material. Large, solid pieces of dry wood will be your main fuel. Smaller twigs or brush are the kindling that keeps the fire going long enough to spread to the main

Start a fire by using dry tinder and small pieces of kindling.

fuel. Finally, you'll need tinder. Tinder is easy to ignite, but it burns very quickly, so it's got to have something to spread to easily.

Starting a fire will be easier if you have waterproof matches, a **butane** lighter (a cigarette lighter), or a kit that uses metals or chemicals to start a fire. Even diehard survivalists like to keep these items on hand, because it makes starting a fire easier and faster. Fortunately, these lightweight items do not take up much room in a backpack, so it's a good idea to have them on hand. If you do not have them, starting a fire will require more time and work, but it is still possible.

One way is to use a lens, such as that from a magnifying glass or a pair of glasses. This will require sunlight. Aim the lens onto your tinder and kindling. As the sun shines through the lens, it will magnify the heat and focus it. When there is enough heat, a small fire will start.

Another way to start a fire is through **friction**. Start with a piece of flat wood to use as the base, or fireboard. Carve a small indentation into it (but not all the way through). Next you'll need a long, round piece of wood to use as a spindle, or drill. You will twist this back and forth into the indentation in the fireboard. The friction from rubbing them together will also create dust and heat. When it gets hot enough, a fire can start. You can use your hands to twist the spindle, but this is very difficult. The bow drill method is more efficient. To make a bow drill, loop a rope around the spindle and another piece of slightly curved wood (the bow). Put a piece of wood on top of the spindle to press down on with your other hand. (This increases the pressure and friction.) Finally, pull the bow back and forth to make the rope turn the spindle. The drier the wood, the easier it will be to create a fire. You can also experiment with different types of wood to see which ones work best.

Drink Up

Water is the next primary need to address. Rainwater and dew are good choices. They are usually pure and safe to drink. You can collect rain and dew in containers, or gather them from the area around you. Water may collect in indentations in rocks or in the folds of leaves. Nature has a lot of nooks and crannies, so look in all of them!

Depending on the area you are in, there may also be rivers or lakes to get water from. Often, this water will not look very clean. It will have dirt and small pieces of plants or other material in it. Your first step is to strain the water. If you have a container, put the water in it and let it stand for a while to let the pieces settle to the bottom. Then you can pour the cleaner water off the top. Next, filter the water. Rocks, sand, charcoal from a fire, and cloth are good filtering materials. Try the sock method. Layer materials into a sock, putting the small, fine materials into the toe of the sock, and working up so that the larger, coarser materials are at the top. For example, put sand at the bottom, then charcoal, then larger pebbles. Now pour the water slowly through. Try to repeat the process several times. This process will remove more impurities, and improve the water's taste.

Filtering by itself is not enough to make the water safe, however. Bacteria live in water, and many of them can make people sick. There are a few ways to purify water. One is to bring water-purifying tablets with you. Iodine or chlorine will do the job. Another good option is to boil the water for several minutes, which will kill the bacteria. If you cannot boil the water, put it in a transparent plastic bottle or bag. Lay it in the sun for several hours. The sun will heat the water and kill many (if not all) of the bacteria.

Finding Food

ood is one of the farthest things down the priority list of things that people actually need during a survival situation. However, the thought of going hungry is bad enough, and once you start feeling hungry it is even worse. Even though you can live without food for a while, it certainly makes you feel better, and it does increase your energy. Most places have some source of food. There are animals, fish, insects and grubs, and plants. The tricky part is figuring out how to get that food—and then determining whether it is safe to eat.

Wooded areas are often full of small animals such as rabbits, squirrels, and birds. It's not necessary to have a gun to kill these animals; instead, they can be captured in traps or snares. However, keep in mind that this may be illegal unless you are on private land (or really starving).

STAYING HEALTHY

It's no fun to be sick, and that is especially true if you are stuck in the wilderness without chicken soup, warm blankets, and TV! With the demands of survival on your body, it is also much easier to get sick or injured. It is important not to neglect any problem, even if it seems minor. A small cut can get infected, so clean and bandage it immediately. If you get a blister from walking, stop to treat it (and take a break from walking!). Although you will not be able to take a hot shower, take the time to keep your body, hair, and clothes as clean as possible. This keeps bugs away and helps prevent infections. Improvise brushing your teeth by chewing on a small (non-poisonous!) twig. Of course, you may have to deal with more serious problems such as hypothermia, frostbite, burns, broken bones, or bleeding, so it's a good idea to learn basic first aid before you set out.

Grubs look gross, but their protein might save your life.

The same goes for fish. If you want to catch your own food, research the different methods that work best on different kinds of animals. It will take practice to build effective traps and know where to place them.

What about creepy crawlies? Most people feel a little sick at the thought of eating bugs, slugs, and worms, but if you can get over the "ick" factor, they can be a good source of food (as long as they are not poisonous). They are high in fat and protein—just the things your body needs to fight the elements.

Foraging for wild plants sounds easy—after all, how hard is it to pick a few berries off a bush? Just as with other tasks in the wild, this is more difficult than it sounds. In general, the farther from the equator you are, the fewer edible plants there are to choose from. The ones that are edible are often only available in the spring or summer. The other problem is knowing what is poisonous and what isn't. Unless you are knowledgeable about what is safe and what isn't, ***do not eat it***. Your body can survive much longer without food than it can if you accidentally eat something toxic.

Learning to live off the land is a long process. Plan to spend a lot of time studying how, when, and where to find and prepare food in the wild. In the meantime, don't start a hike or camping trip without some extra food. If you do get in trouble, you can ration it to last for several extra days.

Never eat wild mushrooms unless you have studied what is safe and what is not.

TEXT-DEPENDENT QUESTIONS

1. In general, how long does it take to get hypothermia in extremely cold weather?

2. What are two ways to start a fire?

3. Why do you need to filter water, such as through sand or the "sock" method?

RESEARCH PROJECT

Look on the Internet to find different types of shelters that can be built in different environments. What would work best for the area you live in?

Making a Shelter

CHAPTER 3

Get Great Gear

ou've spent a couple of weeks planning, and now you're ready to head out for a long weekend in the wilderness. You've practiced some survival skills and know how to use them. And you've packed your backpack with brand-new cool equipment that arrived in the mailbox just in time.

What's wrong here?

 WORDS TO UNDERSTAND

antibiotic able to kill bacteria

essential necessary

LED a type of light that is very efficient and lasts a long time

magnesium a chemical element that lights on fire easily

27

When you are in a survival situation, you are up against the unknown. In this case, untested equipment is a big unknown. Always try things out in advance to make sure you know how to use them and that they work properly.

Backpack Basics

ery few people end up in the wilderness with no supplies at all. Most survival situations happen because something went wrong during a planned hiking or backpacking trip. The good news is that if you planned ahead and packed smart, you should have several **essential** items that you need.

A good sleeping bag that is designed for cold weather should be one of the first items. A camp stove is another useful item. These run on different types of fuel. Research the different kinds and choose the one that will work best for the trips you normally take. Camp stoves are small and fairly light, usually only a couple of pounds.

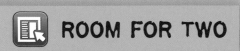

ROOM FOR TWO

Are you repeating yourself? In survival situations, it's a good idea. Consider what things you will have to do, and then make sure you have a couple of tools (at least) to help do those things. For example, it may seem like overkill to bring magnesium firestarter sticks and a butane lighter. But if you lose one, you will be happy you have a backup method. It's also a good idea to pack things that can be used for more than one purpose. Keep in mind that simpler items are usually more versatile.

A small, gas-canister camp stove makes creating hot meals easy.

Beyond that, you will also want to pack your own survival kit. These can be purchased pre-made, but it is usually a better idea to make your own. That way you can include good quality items, and ones that will work best for the environment you will be in.

Don't think about things. When you are in the wilderness, the most important "thing" is action. When you are packing, think about what you would have to do to help yourself survive, and pack items that will let you do them effectively. Keep in mind the area you will be in (such as mountains or desert), as well as the season and possible weather conditions. Put the most important things at the top of the list, and work down from there. Most survivalists agree on a core list of items that are absolute necessities in a survival kit. These include:

- *Firestarters*. Matches do not work if they get wet, and they can only be used once. Instead, try a butane lighter or **magnesium** firestarting sticks.

- *Cotton balls*. These are small and light, and make good tinder material. You can also use lint from the dryer.

- *Water purification tablets*. These take up very little room, and can be stirred into water to kill bacteria and make it safe.

- *Knife*. A quality, sharp knife may be the survivalist's best friend. It works for cutting wood, cleaning fish or animals, and other tasks.

A good knife, a small lantern, some rope, a compass . . . good stuff for a survival kit.

- *Duct tape*. This can be used when building shelters or tools, and makes a great bandage in a pinch. You won't need the whole roll—wrap some around a smaller core to save space.

- *Fishing line and hook*. Not just for fishing! The line can be used to tie things together, and the hook could be used as a makeshift drill.

- *First aid supplies*. Take an emergency stock of painkillers, **antibiotic** ointment, and gauze.

- *Mirror*. This can be used to reflect the sun and signal for help. The larger the surface, the better the signal, so get one that is at least 2x3 inches (5x7.6 cm).

- *Aluminum foil*. Fold up a few sheets into small squares. Foil can be used as a reflective signal (if you've lost the mirror).

- *Whistle*. Can be used to signal for help. It's easier on your lungs, and the sound travels farther. Get it in metal—plastic breaks too easily.

- *Small LED flashlight*. Choose a long-lasting flashlight in a white or yellow color, which can be seen for a longer distance than red.

- *Compass*. A small, extra-thin compass will keep you pointed in the right direction.

- *Cord or rope*. Can also be used for fishing, bundling supplies together for carrying, or supporting parts of a shelter.

- *Small ziplock plastic bags*. Use these to protect your supplies from moisture. The bag can also be used to hold water.

- *Large garbage bags*. A garbage bag can be used as a raincoat, or a waterproof tarp for the roof of your shelter. Plastic is a good insulator, so a bag can double as a blanket. Spread them out to collect rainwater or dew for drinking. Get them in bright orange to increase your chances of being spotted during a rescue.

Compared to the great outdoors, even a large backpack does not hold much. Whenever possible, use the materials and tools that nature has provided. If the ground is covered with dry pine needles and leaves, use those as tinder

for the fire, and save your cotton balls. Vines or other plant materials can be twisted together to make a rope. Wood is possibly the most available tool in nature. With a knife, you can sharpen a piece of wood into a spear for fishing or use a stick as a fishing pole. Stones can be used to sharpen knives, construct solid shelters or fire pits, and used as hammers.

Dressing for Survival

What you wear into the wilderness is one of the most important decisions you make. Of course, you want to dress appropriately for the region and the season, but if the weather changes, you want to be ready. Layers of clothing let you peel off or bundle up as necessary. You can switch out your clothing and always have something dry to wear, especially at night when the temperature drops.

Sweat is your enemy in a survival situation. Even if it is cold out, you may sweat when you are working. As soon as you slow down, your body stops producing excess heat. As sweat dries, it takes your body heat with it. Some types of fabric, such as cotton, stay wet much longer than others, and will chill you fast. Natural materials like wool are a better choice. There are a lot of high-tech fabrics out there that are lightweight and waterproof. These can be good in short-term situations, but they are not as durable as natural materials. They may also burn or melt, which makes them dangerous around fires. A combination of fabrics and weights is the best way to go.

It's possible to use many items of clothing as makeshift tools, as well. Shoelaces can be used to hold a bandage in place—and you can make that bandage from a sock or a strip of cloth from a shirt. Almost any type of non-waterproof cloth will work to filter water. A metal zipper from a pair of pants can act as a small saw. A belt can be used to tie sticks of wood together to make them easier to carry. The metal prong in the buckle may be used as a sharp point for drilling. In a pinch, you can

Knowing some basic first aid is a good plan when heading for an adventure.

use bits of your clothes to help start a fire, but remember, your clothes are your first line of defense against the elements. The most important thing they do is protect your body. Do not ruin them unless there is no other option.

Making sure to have a head covering can be important, too, especially in hot, sunny places. If you don't have a hat, you can make a covering from large leaves or you can weave together thin strands of plant materials into a shade covering to put on your head.

Keeping a positive attitude if you're lost or alone will help greatly.

The most important thing to remember is that it's not *what* you're carrying—it's how you use it. In a survival situation, the traditional rules don't apply. Train yourself to be creative, and if it works, go for it!

TEXT-DEPENDENT QUESTIONS

1. Why should you test your equipment before going on a trip?

2. How can aluminum foil help in a survival situation?

3. What is one way you could use an item of clothing for another job?

RESEARCH PROJECT

Find several lists of items that are recommended for survival kits. Which things always make the list? Which ones would you consider "extras"? Try to make your own survival kit that could fit into a container the size of a coffee mug.

Backpack Basics

Survival expert Bear Grylls

CHAPTER 4

Further Adventures

n television shows, survivalists do some amazing—and sometimes pretty gross—things. They may wrestle alligators, eat slugs, or walk around in the snow wearing only their socks. These "reality" shows, however, are sometimes not very realistic. True survival takes a lot longer than an hour with commercial breaks. Plus, if these guys get into real trouble, there is usually someone to rescue them. In a real survival situation, of course, you are on your own. In addition to the basic skills covered earlier in this book, there are also more advanced ways to prepare yourself.

 WORDS TO UNDERSTAND

orient to determine the proper direction

resources materials and skills that can be useful in survival situations

trench a long hole or pit dug into the ground that serves as protection

Know Your Environment

N o one usually expects to be in a survival situation, and it is difficult to plan for the unexpected. On any trip, you should have some idea of your surroundings. Before going on a camping or hiking trip, take the time to study up on the area you'll be in. If possible, before you venture into an unfamiliar place, go out with a local resident who knows the area. They can give you tips about helpful skills and other **resources** on the land.

Every environment will have its own advantages and disadvantages. For example, it should be easy to find water if you are trapped in the snow. All you have to do is eat it, right? Well yes—and no. If you eat too

Surviving means being creative with the tools around you.

A sudden sandstorm can send even the hardiest riders scrambling for cover.

much snow you will get hypothermia. The key is to melt it first, so it does not chill your insides.

Other regions have their own challenges. In a rainforest, would you know to look up (as well as down) to keep an eye out for poisonous snakes that live in trees? Would you know which plants were edible and which to stay away from? In the desert, would you know to dig a **trench** into the sand to protect yourself during a sandstorm? On the open ocean, would you know that you can get water from the insides of fish?

These environments are some of the most hostile and forbidding on the planet. However, they are all survivable—at least for a time—if you've learned what they have to offer.

Lost? Your first move is to use a compass to orient yourself.

Finding Your Place

I t can be exciting to head out into the great unknown. You wonder what's around the next bend in the path, or over the next hill. However, it is easy for an adventure to go wrong. One step in the wrong direction leads to two. Before you know it you are hopelessly lost. This happens even to people who are used to being in the outdoors. In their heads, they have a mental map of where they think they are. They find it comforting to follow this map, even when their surroundings should tell them it is wrong! If you do get lost, throw out your mental map. Pay attention to what is really around you.

Survival Ideas

Not many places on Earth are completely unexplored, even if it feels like you're in the most remote corner of the globe. There are probably maps that provide at least some general information. Learn where major natural landmarks are, such as rivers or mountains. Note where the closest towns or campgrounds are in relation to those landmarks. The landmarks can help you keep your bearings if you are lost, and will help guide you back to civilization.

A thin compass is easy to carry with you, and can point you in the right general direction. If you do not have a compass, there are still ways to **orient** yourself. Nature has a lot of clues that can help you figure out where you are. Obviously, the sun rises in the east and sets in the west. The star Polaris is also called the North Star because it hangs right above the North Pole. If you know even some basic astronomical facts and features, you can begin to figure out where you are on Earth. Study in advance, though: it's pretty easy to identify the sun, but other stars can be a little harder.

Sometimes the sky is not helpful. If it is raining or cloudy, there may not be enough signs overhead. Then you can use other clues. Plants and trees, for example, usually grow toward the sun. An exception is moss. Moss grows better in cool, shady areas. Moss on trees will usually grow on the side opposite from the sun.

Not all rules apply all the time, though. Sometimes moss grows on all sides of a tree. Maybe the wind has forced trees to grow in a particular direction. Use several clues together with one another. With a few bits of information, you can begin to piece together your location and direction.

A big decision in a survival situation is whether to try to walk out, or to stay in one place. You may have to keep moving in order to find shelter or water, or you may have gone missing in a place no one will think to look. In those cases, pick a direction to travel and stick with it. If you roam around aimlessly, you may return to a place rescuers already

Looking for attention? If you are lost, you should be! If you can see or hear rescuers nearby, you may be able to call out or blow a whistle that gets their attention. In most cases, however, you will probably be too far away to be heard. That's the time for a visual signal. A signal fire can be seen from miles away and from above. The smoke from the fire also tells rescuers where you are. Another way is to flash sunlight off a reflective material, such as a mirror or a square of aluminum foil (pictured). This bright flash can be seen as far as 50 miles away. Aim your target in the direction that potential rescuers would be coming from. Do it several times in a row to create a deliberate pattern that people will recognize.

looked. If possible, follow a river or stream (moving downstream). Water flows downhill, and is more likely to take you back to civilization.

On the other hand, sometimes it is best to stay put. You may be injured, or the weather may be too bad to travel in. If someone knows the general idea of where you went and will get worried when you don't come back on time, it is best to wait it out. Build a shelter, wear your brightest clothes, and keep your signal fire going.

It's All in Your Head

t's a scary thought to be stranded in the wilderness. Even people who are used to the outdoors can panic and make bad decisions. They may start to lose hope that they will find their way out or that someone will rescue them. They can lose confidence in their abilities to do the things that will keep them alive. It is common to feel angry and frustrated, or to blame yourself for getting into a bad situation. None of this helps. After you get back to safety, you can think about what went wrong and what you could have done better. But for now, it's about getting through.

So, give yourself a little pep talk that focuses on staying calm and using your head. Do not plunge ahead without knowing what you are doing. Instead, take a few minutes to stop and make a plan. Do not get too worried about all the things that you *should* do. Do not get hung up on what *might* happen. Take it step by step. Figure out what the most important thing to do is. Then do it. Now move on to the next thing. Of course, you may not be able to accomplish everything you want to—at least not at first. Stay positive by focusing on what you *can* do—and keep working on the other problems.

The key to survival in an outdoor situation is to remain calm . . . and think.

Whether you are in a true survival situation or just want to give yourself a challenge, having some basic skills and a few key supplies goes a long way. Put them together with some smart thinking, and you may find that you know more than how to survive in the wild—you can thrive there.

Plan ahead and use teamwork, and you'll be able to face any challenge.

TEXT-DEPENDENT QUESTIONS

1. How can plants or trees help you determine what direction you are facing?

2. If you are lost, when should you stay where you are and wait for rescuers?

3. What are two ways to signal for help?

 RESEARCH PROJECT

Read up on some true survival situations in extreme environments, such as snow or the open sea. Find out what people did to survive, and how they used skills that were good for those places.

FIND OUT MORE

WEBSITES

www.wildwoodsurvival.com/
Check out this site for lots of information on survival skills and supplies.

www.survivenature.com/
This page offers some basic tips for surviving in a variety of extreme environments.

www.wildernesscollege.com/basic-survival-skills.html
Mental attitude, priorities, and links to practical skills are covered on this page.

BOOKS

Ellar, Simon. *Survival Skills: How to Survive in the Wild*. Mankato, MN: Capstone, 2011.

Long, Denise. *Survivor Kid: A Practical Guide to Wilderness Survival*. Chicago: Chicago Review Press, 2011.

Towell, Colin. *The Survival Handbook: Essential Skills for Outdoor Adventure*. New York: DK, 2012.

bushcraft wilderness skills, named for the remote bush country of Australia

camouflage a pattern or disguise in clothing designed to make it blend into the surroundings

conservation the act of preserving or protecting, such as an environment or species

ecosystem the habitats of species and the ways that species interact with each other

friction the resistance that happens when two surfaces rub together

insulation protection from something, such as extreme hot or cold

layering adding layers of clothing to stay warm and removing layers to cool off.

rewilding returning to a more natural state

synthetic man-made, often to imitate a natural material

traction the grip or contact that an object has with another surface

wake the waves produced by the movement of a boat

INDEX

PHOTO CREDITS

(Dreamstime.com: DT. Dollarphoto.com: Dollar) Tyler Olson/DT 6; Candybox Images/DT 9; Miloszg/DT 10; Ammit/DT 12; Warrengoldswain/DT 15; Galyna Andrushko/DT 16; Maxim Shebeko/DT 18; .shock/DT 20; Yodke67/DT 23; Vorclub/DT 24; Martinmark/DT 26, 38; Paketesama/DT 28; Alexei Novikov/DT 29; Tab1962/DT 30; Robyn MacKenzie/DT 31t; Mikhail Koknanchikov/DT 31b; Johann Helgason/DT 32; Kaninstudio/Dollar 33; Illustrissima/Dollar 34; Courtesy Bear Grylls Ventures/Flickr 36; Donsimon/DT 39; Photographerlondon/DT 40; Michael L. Haas/USMC; endostock/Dollar; Vitalalp/DT.

ABOUT THE AUTHOR

Diane Bailey has written about 50 nonfiction books for kids and teens, on topics ranging from science to sports to celebrities. Diane also works as a freelance editor, helping authors who write novels for children and young adults. Diane has two sons and two dogs, and lives in Kansas.